Donalie Hartwell

VANTAGE PRESS
New York

FIRST EDITION

Copyright © 1993, 1995 by Donalie Hartwell

Published by Vantage Press, Inc.
516 West 34th Street, New York, New York 10001

Manufactured in the United States of America
ISBN: 0-533-11501-9

Library of Congress Catalog Card No.: 95-90202

0 9 8 7 6 5 4 3 2

Dedication

To Dalbert, Albert, "Zippy Squir-rel Esquire", for choosing to always allow me to be me, and loving me unconditionally

Acknowledgements

- Many thanks to KEVIN O'CONNOR for his expertise and wizardry on the computer. His incredible patience and sense of humour made working with him a joy.

- Thank you's to LOUIS ZIMMERMAN and JANE CARR DESIGN for their help in the creation of the drawings; the title, the roses and the butterfly.

- Much gratitude to DALBERT HARTWELL for the front and back cover photography.

Life Is Like A Restaurant... FULL OF CHOICES

Life is an endless stream of choices and decisions which lead us to and from our victories and defeats. Thus, what we choose for our lives affects not only external but internal conditions as well.

Nature mirrors and teaches us in very interesting ways. There is a great parallel to life in the choices we make at a restaurant or in our kitchen. These choices lead to internal and external appearances just as our life choices do.

Philosophers, theologians, metaphysicians and even medical scientists are getting on board with the idea that choices in our thoughts affect our feelings and health, just as our food choices do. How we fine tune our choices, both in life and the restaurant, or kitchen, can dictate our outcome in living a happy, healthy and productive life. We can be like the rabbit in Alice in Wonderland, "no time to say hello, good-bye I'm late, I'm late, I'm late". Or, we can say "don't worry, be happy". Another choice is we can be cool, calm and collected, for we do choose our own reality.

For example, let's say you walk into a restaurant, are seated and given a menu. The server appears, you ask for some eggs, bread and juice. Off the server goes and brings back hard boiled eggs, rye toast and orange juice. You look at the food and say "I do not like hard boiled eggs, I wanted scrambled, and rye toast gives me hives, and orange juice is too acidic for my system." Is it the server's fault that you were not clear and precise about what you wished to eat? Of course not! The responsibility for yours, mine or anyone's life is strictly on our own shoulders. If we get this concept in its totality, and it sinks in at a level where we take responsibility for our outcomes, both in life and decisions in a restaurant or kitchen, then a balance of peace, joy and friction is in the making.

This book is dedicated to helping you live your life on your own terms, and living your life with freely given choices—choices made without guilt or fear as the primary motivator. I personally hope that this also conveys a freedom from thoughts that, unless your life is full of sunshine, hearts and flowers it is not a good one. It is my firm belief that friction, discord, unhappiness, etc. are to be dealt with in the same manner as you might feel winning a million dollar lottery or windfall.

An attitude of gratitude is essential no matter what befalls you. Giving praise for all of life's ups and downs allows the healing to take place in our lives. As hard as that may sound, when we all do this our happiness quotient rises.

When we all learn, myself included, that we must meet life with joy, happiness and a positive outlook, whether good or bad is coming our way, then we will truly live at a level of consciousness which can embrace that"Peace that passeth understanding", which is so often sought after, and very seldom experienced in life.

We all get glimpses of that "Peace" from time to time in many different ways. Sometimes a selection of music speaks to us and lifts us out of our bondage of cares and woes, and for a moment, a heartbeat or two, we experience utter peace of mind and body. Often, a beautiful picture, artwork, landscapes of majestic proportions or simple beauty give us that "Peace". The closeness one feels with their family, spouse, children, loved ones, friends or their deity such as God, Allah, Jehovah, just to name a few, brings them that fleeting "Peace" we all seek. In searching for that "Peace" we all want it to last forever.

It is my contention that on this planet called Earth, we human beings are like complex computers capable of being programmed by ourselves or others to make choices; good, bad or indifferent.

Our challenge is to direct those choices from within. We all have our quiet thoughts and our own inner small voice that gives us direction. Some feel this is God's gentle prodding, guiding us towards our Divine Plan.

Not all of our lives should be programmed for total "Peace" all the time. Our growth, both inner and outer, would then be in a vacuum, a static-like state not allowing friction or discord to push us along in our lessons and learning. Just as children must learn to eat, walk, talk and make their way through decision making programming by themselves, and with help from others, the same is true for everyone else from young men and women to senior citizens. They must learn the same way. Some call it trial and error. The learning never stops. It's often said that the wiser we get, the more we know we don't know.

Friction or discord is the force that allows us to know the difference between turbulence, upsets, unhappiness and "Peace". We should learn to welcome our trials and tribulations because they allow us to grow and rise and make progress to not only understand ourselves and our loved ones, but LIFE.

It is my belief that, FRICTION IS NECESSARY, for our growth. Notice I did not say a necessary evil. In pure thought, evil does not exist; neither does right or wrong. We simply qualify feelings and thoughts to that end. What is evil or bad is simply energy we qualify, and we alone decide how our choices to qualify that energy affect our lives. This does not mean we can justify acting outside of our integrity, or the highest intention of unconditional love. That small, quiet voice we all hear inside our mind, and very seldom listen to, will always give us our guidance.

I have given permission to my quiet voice to be very loud if I do not listen to its gentle prodding. When we are in touch with ourselves and not separate from who we are, we can never experience loneliness. We truly become our own best friend.

Nature, I think, is a great teacher. Let us take the beautiful rose and butterfly as examples. Their end outcomes are "Peace", beauty and perfection. However, their journeys to get there are full of friction and great risk.

Let us take the rose first, one of the most fragrant and beautiful flowers, in an endless variety of hues, scents and forms. We use this flower to express our highest emotions and thoughts when we give it to others. BUT, how did that flower come to be such a blessing to us?

A seed is planted into the soil. The seed is nourished with food, which we hope was well chosen to do its best for the rose, thus allowing the rose to have a beautiful outcome. The seed, after having partaken of the nourishment, has to grow, fight the soil with its rocks and insects, and push itself through the underground soil, black and dank. It works through all manner of problems such as rocks, bugs and chemicals to rise above, to reach outside that dirt towards the light of the outer atmosphere.

It finally emerges, not as a flower, but

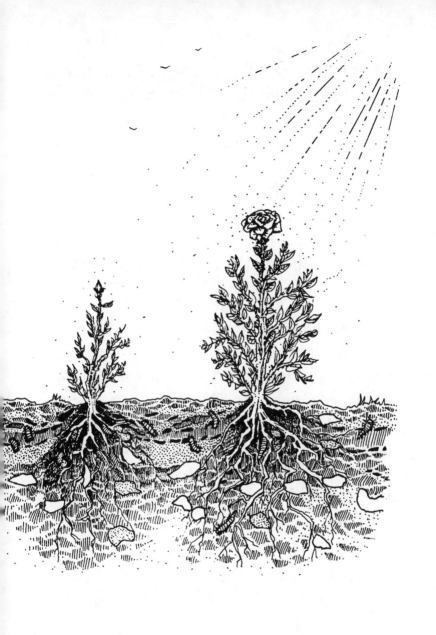

many times a plant with thorns. These thorns stick anything that touches them, not causing pleasure but pain. These thorns grow on the outgrowth of that seed known as the stem. As it goes through its life cycle, that seed/stem makes a place for the blossom, the "rose", to emerge and bless us all. You might say the thorns protect the rose's crowning glory, its blossom—the highest expression of the seed.

Legends and myths of love and tragedy have been written and lived around this fragrant and delicate beauty that words cannot do justice to describe. The rose evokes feelings deep within us when we simply glance at its magnificent splendor. When we look at the human personality, we can see how its thorn-like peccadilloes similarly may protect our beautiful loving side.

Have we not met someone in our lives who is brusque, gruff and hard, only to find when we get to know them, they have a very soft, nice, almost vulnerable side, and would do anything for us? Sometimes we need to get past the thorns in life to discover the beauty in it.

Did the seed start out with the finally formed beautiful rose? The idea of that beautiful flower was in the seed from the very beginning. The seed was programmed to its destiny, a beautiful flower that gives pleasure with its blossom and pain with its thorns. Both "Peace" and friction existed to allow that seed, which flowered, to grow and protect itself along the way. Had there not been friction to help press upon the seed, it would never have pushed its stem higher and higher out of the soil, into the light, so the sun could nourish it and assist its growth.

We all can relate to some bad experience we have had, which at the time, seemed very hard and unhappy. Later, sometimes years later, we look back and say "that was the best thing that ever could have happened to me". This can be events like fights with people, divorce, firings from jobs or illness, just to name a few.

Those events took us out of our everyday state of mind, perhaps even our complacency, and propelled us to look at things differently. This often helps us evaluate our choices, and hence the direction of our lives changes. The friction or discord of those situations pushed us to grow.

Just as some roses grow faster than others, so do some people learn from unhappiness faster. The point is, we need friction to grow.

As the car's tires can't go down the road without friction, so does the seed not grow without friction's assistance or the human being not progress without it.

Thus the beautiful rose would not exist if it was not pushed towards its ultimate outcome. The rose becomes its perfect expression by feeding, friction, nurturing, care and even love, just as the human being becomes the beautiful being it is, was and always will be by feeding, friction, nurturing, care and love. However, should we not water the rose, prune it, fertilize it and help protect it from the elements, pests, weather, stomping feet, etc., we will cause it to wither, die and hence not turn out to be the beautiful rose it was intended to be. We must nurture, feed, love and care for us human beings with the same dedication as the gardener tends the rose.

As the rose-seed worked so hard against friction under the surface of the dirt, no one could see or appreciate how hard it was trying, just to simply be. It received no comments on its beauty. No one knew it existed underneath the soil but the one who planted it and tended its garden. Do we not feel impatient for that rose to grow and blossom to the beauty it is? Do we not feel impatient about our growth or that of others we know? Just as the rose does not get praised for its inside/ hidden effort as it grows, we human beings are often treated likewise. And yes, we are also very impatient with ourselves for not growing and becoming the wonderful person we can be. We also often get discouraged with the lack of progress in ourselves.

I firmly believe that if we will just push on and press a little harder, knowing we all have that beautiful expression like the rose in us, we will find our place in the sun along the way. We will also discover our inner and outer beauty. I believe that all problems can be solved with enough conversation, paperwork and patience.

Remember the expression "beauty is in the eye of the beholder". Just as some prefer white, red, yellow or mauve roses, some prefer different human characteristics and expressions. All roses are beautiful in their own right, and so are human beings. Each person is given a vehicle, a body which expresses different features, colors and personalities.

These different features make us as beautiful a hue as a rainbow of roses. No one has the right to say one rose is better or more beautiful than another. The rose is simply its perfect expression, just as each human being is a perfect expression of its seed.

We would learn well not to be so judgmental or intolerant of others' differences, and be more grateful for the beauty of their diversities. Each person brings a wonderful uniqueness to the rainbow of life.

What sets us human beings apart from all other forms of life is our **free will**. We are supposed to be a higher order. I long for the day when we can look around the world and see our free will used to love our fellow human beings, giving them a right to be and worship, however their free will allows them, without judgment because they are different. THAT WOULD BE GROWTH!

This does not mean that everyone should have the right to do anything they wish to another human being. In order to coexist on this planet, we should respect peoples' space and free will. However, to survive as a group, society must govern itself with conduct for the betterment of all. I believe the friction and discord of the world teaches us, through man's inhumanity to man, that we, the highest order with all of our free will, need to grow into that title "higher order".

We will then become the expression, both inside and out, of balance and beauty.

This will allow us to live our lives in a thirty three and a third percent ratio of balance being LOVE, WISDOM AND POWER. These qualities will guide and empower us to our highest expression as human beings.

Love, without wisdom and power to guide it, is unempowered and unattained in its highest expression. Wisdom without the direction of love and power is unactualized. Power without love and wisdom to govern it can bring down the human condition and environment crushing all in its path. Therefore BALANCE is the key in all things.

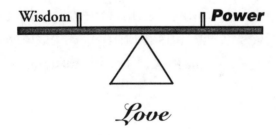

Whether in life, in the restaurant or in the kitchen, balanced choices nurture us, and our free will then serves our learning to its greatest potential. If we eat only sweets and starches, our physical body inside and out will not function in the balance we would like. If we eat fruits, vegetables, carbohydrates and starches, and yes, even sweets in a balanced manner, we will function much better.

Learning and growth are limitless; they have no boundaries. We let our judgments shorten our vision. Life is like a kaleidoscope of various colors, shapes and sizes, all determined by how we turn the kaleidoscope. This gives us various mixtures of patterns, as the choices we make in life give us a particular outcome.

Just as we looked at the rose, let us ponder the butterfly. What a magnificent, delicate expression of life; a myriad of color, texture, shape and variety. It starts from the egg as what some might call an ugly bug. It appears cumbersome to itself, and to others, all wrapped up in itself and its journey through life, to become a magnificent spectacle of perfection. This transformation may seem improbable, to say the least. The hard work the caterpillar does inside the cocoon, for what may appear as a short life span when it emerges (from days to weeks), may seem futile. However, the full expression of beauty this bug displays as the mature butterfly, in its delicate perfection, is rare.

This should give us pause for encouragement and great joy. If a bug can overcome this great obstacle, we, as the higher order, should be able to breeze through our trials and tribulations to show our beautiful magnificent inner and outer selves. Here's a part of life, the caterpillar, whose appearance before it emerges from the cocoon is not as pretty, perhaps, as its end result—the butterfly. However, it plods on growing and growing, stretching through friction and peace to become what it knows it is, was, and always will be— BEAUTIFUL!

Can we not learn from the caterpillar/ butterfly and work pushing ourselves through all our stages of growth, until we reach our potential—a beautiful expression, a human being, full of love, wisdom and power to all we meet and greet?

How do we begin the transformation to become our own beautiful rose and butterfly? We simply decide, to choose, to be.

Using our free will, which remember makes us a higher order, we can decide and program our mind and body however we choose. We can choose to be as happy, healthy and successful as we want, or we can choose to be miserable. Remember, we are the Captain of our own ship of life. We decide how to set our sails for fair or stormy weather. Just as a ship is designed to sail the ocean's open and unknown waters, so are the human beings' physical, mental and emotional bodies designed to weather life.

We decide if we let our feelings get hurt with pride, envy, gossip or other discords. We decide if we choose to let our race, creed, age, gender or color dictate our outcomes and state of mind, good or bad. We decide when or if we want to grow and be instinctively what each person inside knows they can be, simply beautiful.

We, as human beings decide how much Love, Wisdom and Power we want in our lives. We then decide how to balance the teeter-totter of life. This balance will bring all the joy and prosperity we can dream of for our lives. If we let unconditional love be the fulcrum of the teeter-totter, then all our decisions will be guided by the example of the beautiful rose and butterfly. Love guides wisdom and power to their best and highest expressions. Again, **we** decide our outcome.

Just as you go to a restaurant or your kitchen, your menu has choices. If you want eggs you decide on boiled, fried, scrambled, over easy, sunny-side up, deviled or omeletted, etc. When you are clear in your needs, wants and desires, you will make a choice that fits. This applies in life, just as it does in food choices. We make choices in our lives which either add to or take away from our ultimate goal of being the best we can be.

We can choose the path. We can blame others for our plight. We can be miserable and say "POOR ME", which may lead to unhappiness, ill health and poverty. We can also choose to live our lives in conversation with ourselves and others saying "I could have, I should have". Just as the ship's sails handle the forces of nature, so do we, through our choices, handle the forces of our lives.

One can say "HEY! I AM THE CAPTAIN OF MY SHIP—I'LL DECIDE WHAT HAPPENS TO IT, NOT THE HE SAID'S, SHE SAID'S, OR OTHER OF LIFE'S HAPPENINGS".

This allows you to Captain your life in the direction you choose, and not be driven by any external conditions which may befall you. No human being is less than any other. We are all on a level playing field, and we choose individually what happens to us. We decide our fate to live as victim, martyr or Captain of our ship to our own best wishes, desires and aspirations.

At this point a lot of people might say "yeah, but you don't know my problems", "but you couldn't possibly understand my troubles"— BOO HOO! BOO HOO! Remember, each of us decides our own life. The choices of envy, greed, avarice, self-pity, enslavement to wants, seeming needs and desires are all choices you control. You can decide how to achieve what you want in your life and go get it on your own terms.

THE ONLY PERSON WHO CAN TRULY STOP YOU IS SIMPLY ON THE OTHER SIDE OF THE MIRROR.

Self-doubt can cause your decisions to maneuver your ship of life into dangerous waters. Just as a Captain follows a charted course to get to his destination, so do we human beings need to chart or plan our course and direction for our lives. The term often used for this course is our own individual Divine Plan. This will enable us to get to our destination in the most expeditious manner. For example, someone desiring to go from Los Angeles to New York has lots of decisions to make.

A person can choose not to get a map and simply get into a car and start driving. The person may go due West, fall into the ocean and unless rescued, will not make the destination. One can choose no map, head due East and just feel the way, knowing New York is to the Northeast.

They can muddle through by guess and by golly, asking strangers for directions, and by hoping and wishing they may or may not get to New York. It becomes a Don Quixote existence, hoping to tilt at enough windmills, metaphorically speaking, to arrive in New York.

A person could decide to get a map, and if assistance is needed to read and understand that map, get it. Based on that choice, one could chart a course based on a lot of other choices, for example the time of year. Depending on sun or snow, the direction taken from Los Angeles could be through the South to avoid icy roads and mountains.

The amount of time one has determines the choice of route. More time allows for excursions through mountains, valleys, towns and meeting people. One decides the experience of a trip or outcome, just as we decide by choices the outcome of our lives.

The type of transportation also affects the journey. One could choose an airplane, car, train, motorcycle, bicycle, roller-skates, skateboard, surfboard, hot air balloon, boat, wheelchair, crutches, walking or running. Each form of transportation may get you there fully or partway. A combination of several may be needed to reach your destination.

Our careers often decide our life's experiences and growth; the vehicles of the workplace often determine our course in life.

There is no right choice. You choose, depending on what the outcome of your journey is to be for yourself. You decide what matters most in your journey. You can take a no-nonsense direct approach, with few life gathering experiences to reflect upon. You decide how to proceed, knowing within that journey you can still make choices which can change the outcome of your trip. Remember, New York is a state of mind, and how you get to your state of mind is your journey of life. The journey of your life is filled with choices. The choices all affect your state of mind. Your destination is greatly determined by your mindset.

When someone awakes in the morning they begin to choose. One chooses whether to get out of bed, or if they get out, how to proceed with the next choice. Most people make lots of choices from their bed, for example what time to get up, whether to shower or bathe, what clothes to put on (depending upon their day's activities), what breakfast they want to eat and even if they wish to exercise. Not many people write down what they would like to accomplish that day. Those who do, mostly just list the everyday chores of shopping, errands and appointments.

If we were to order our life day by day, just as we order our meal at a restaurant, with clarity, precision and anticipation of fulfillment, **then** we would experience our lives at a much more fulfilling level. How can we expect our life to be what we want, when we do not tell ourselves what we want, minute by minute and day to day, year in and year out? Clarifying our life's direction with goals helps put us on the right track to personal fulfillment.

This doesn't mean we should get unhappy or impatient if we order our life and it is not instantly filled like a restaurant meal. It is my belief this is where faith in ourselves and the outcome of our hard work comes in. Just as a seed takes time to emerge from the soil, so does a human being take time to grow in new directions. As I often say, how does anyone eat anything large, such as an elephant or a pumpkin? "One bite at a time"!

So, *CHOOSE*. Start in motion your ideas. Plan a desired outcome, and remember to be balanced and happy, no matter what befalls you.

Be grateful for all things, good, bad and indifferent. This will allow your journey to be happier and more fruitful. I believe gratitude for everything, big and small, allows life to give you more. However, having gratitude does not mean you cannot Captain your ship of life in any direction you wish. You do not have to accept, as your destination, the storms of life, which may appear as unhappiness, pain, discord or your station in life.

Be grateful for everything. Your destination is **what you choose**. Turn your sails toward hope, faith, happiness, and positivity. Then your plans and choices will steer your life in the direction you choose to go.

Do not allow others to Captain your ship of life. Let them serve as mates to assist in your decisions. Remember, the final direction and course of action is always yours and yours alone. Just as the ocean has many storms and clearings, so does life. There is always another sea to sail, another day to go through. Part of the fun and joy of life is letting it happen, so its great variety can change, surprise and delight you.

Just as you can hold the wheel of the ship too tightly, so can you be too rigid in your thinking. Allow for different routes and ways of getting there. Going doggedly about your way, head down, pushing forward, may get you where you want to go. The cost however, of not seeing the beauty, love, and humanity of your surroundings may be lost. Balance is the byword.

I say you are the Captain of your ship, but remember the mates who are there to help you sail it. There are always people to assist us on our journey, and it is a blessing to ourselves and others to allow them to help. One must learn to be able to give and receive. It is very important to remember to allow others to help us, guide us and support us, but WE must do our own final choices and work.

In my mind human beings are a team. We play on Planet Earth. How we all cooperate, love, work with and even fight with our teammates determines our individual and team success. I firmly believe that just as no two roses or butterflies are alike, no two human beings are alike. This is a wonderful, glorious thing. We are all needed on this team of life in order to fill our team positions. No position is any more important than another. All the bases and field must be covered, in order to win. Then, we can all accomplish our own unique destinations.

This enables us to share our journey. We can live in love, with wisdom and power, and allow our fellow team mates to have as much freedom, joy, fun, happiness and growth as they choose. This allows them to find their own unique destinations.

By the way, because we are a team on Planet Earth, we should wish the best for others, just as we do ourselves. When someone is ill, do we not show caring, gentleness and even forgiveness? People are affected by their everyday cares and woes, which may make them ill. Not perhaps in a physical sense, but they are not as happy, well and prosperous as they might wish to be. They could be suffering from burdens you cannot see.

Wouldn't it be nice if we treated everyone, whether we perceived them as well or ill, with the same kindness, caring and forgiveness and yes, even unconditional love? This Earth and our everyday lives have enough friction naturally without us adding to it through our unkind words or deeds.

Life is an unending journey filled with team players, each Captain of their own lives, allowing other team members the same privileges as they want for themselves. **Life**, giving one and all, through unconditional love, *choices* of being up or down, having friction or growth. **Life**, allowing one and all to become their own beautiful rose and butterfly.

Let everyone be full of unique dimensions, sharing them for the betterment of ourselves and others.

Thank you for choosing to share some time with me, and with my thoughts. I welcome your insights. Go in "Peace" to the beauty you are.

With unconditional love,

Your friend,

Donalie

Donalie

Donalie, the author of *Life is Like a Restaurant...Full of Choices* brings over twenty–six years of business, sales, management, seminar and entrepreneurial experience to all levels of the private and public sectors. She has also worked in higher education, governmental arenas, and as an executive director for an international foundation. She has been helping both established and start–up businesses as well as individuals define and meet their personal and financial goals.

Donalie has incredible energy and enthusiasm, with unique creative problem–solving abilities. Her uniqueness is demonstrated by the fact that she was the first woman hired by a 100–year–old "Fortune 500" company. Then, in less than one year, she became the recipient of the company's most coveted award — "Man of the Year".